EVERYONE BELONGS

Dennis Vanasse, M.Ed.

Illustrated by:
Lyle John Jakosalem

To order additional copies of this book, contact:
Xlibris LLC
1-888-795-4274
www.Xlibris.com
Orders@Xlibris.com

Before I was born, one would dream

Never did they think my life
would be so extreme

A healthy child, worry free

I am really special even though I have EB

I am very tough, I fight, I fight

My skin peels off if
you hold me tight

EB children wonder
Why? Why? Why?

Please remember I'm
happy, no need to cry

2

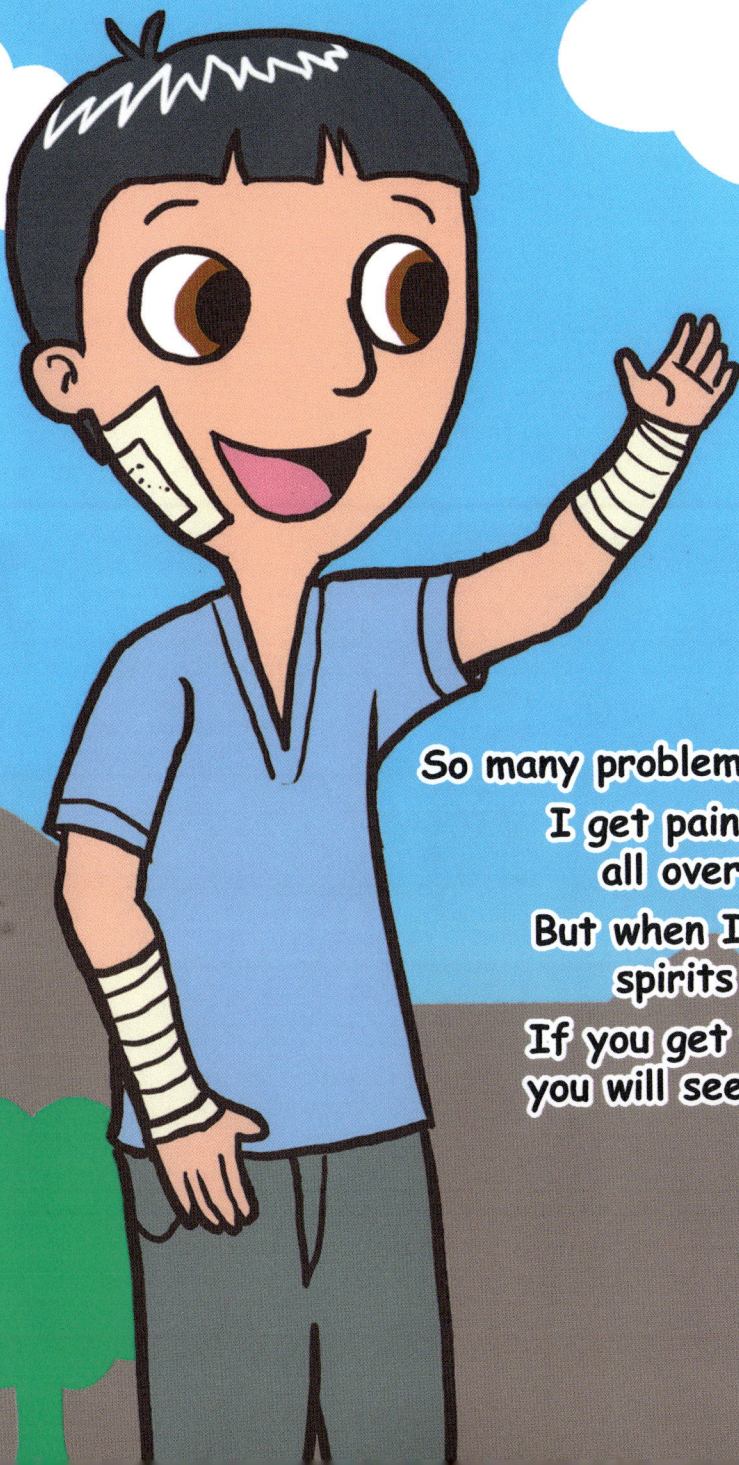

So many problems, where to begin
I get painful blisters
all over my skin
But when I smile, your
spirits will lift
If you get to know me,
you will see I am a gift

3

It hurts my feelings when people stop and stare
Never asked for a disorder that is so rare
Listen to this message that is so true
Just remember, even though I
have EB, I am just like you

24 HOURS

4

Simple things take so long
When my skin gets infected, I must be strong
With research a cure may be near, not too far
Many of my blisters turn into scars

I still need affection, a cuddly hug

Simple, soft-clothing,
please never tug

Kids may be afraid because
they don't understand

If you are gentle, you
can hold my hand

When I fall, I can get an ouchy boo boo
You must know I am unique, just like you
For me I don't want you to ever be sad
Because my sores feel better when I use special pads

When I play t-ball, I feel alive
Please be gentle when you give me a high-five
Since it's too sticky, I won't use a band-aid
I love to eat French fries with blue Gatorade

It's fun to talk on the phone, great
when friends send me a letter

Should stay away from crunchy foods
because softer are much better

Makes my heart skip a beat when
children call me by my name

There are different types of EB, we are not all the same

I can beat you at puzzles, I am really quick
Please be careful around me when you are sick
Once we connect, you won't want to be apart
Guarantee you will love me from the very start

Cannot play outside when it's hot, but still want to belong

My skin may be fragile, but I am so strong

Like many of you, my room is always a mess

Would love to be challenged because I am the king at chess

When I make mistakes, I accept the blame
In school, would love for you to know my name
I paint pictures, stories I write
Just give me a chance, I am so polite

RYAN K3

Why me I ask? It is not fair
This story I tell to make you aware
My skin is so fragile, I must avoid the heat
Making friends makes my life so complete

Sometimes I'm in pain and don't feel good
I know my sister would make me feel better if she could
Please always ask questions and don't assume
I might have a nurse or a helper in the classroom

14

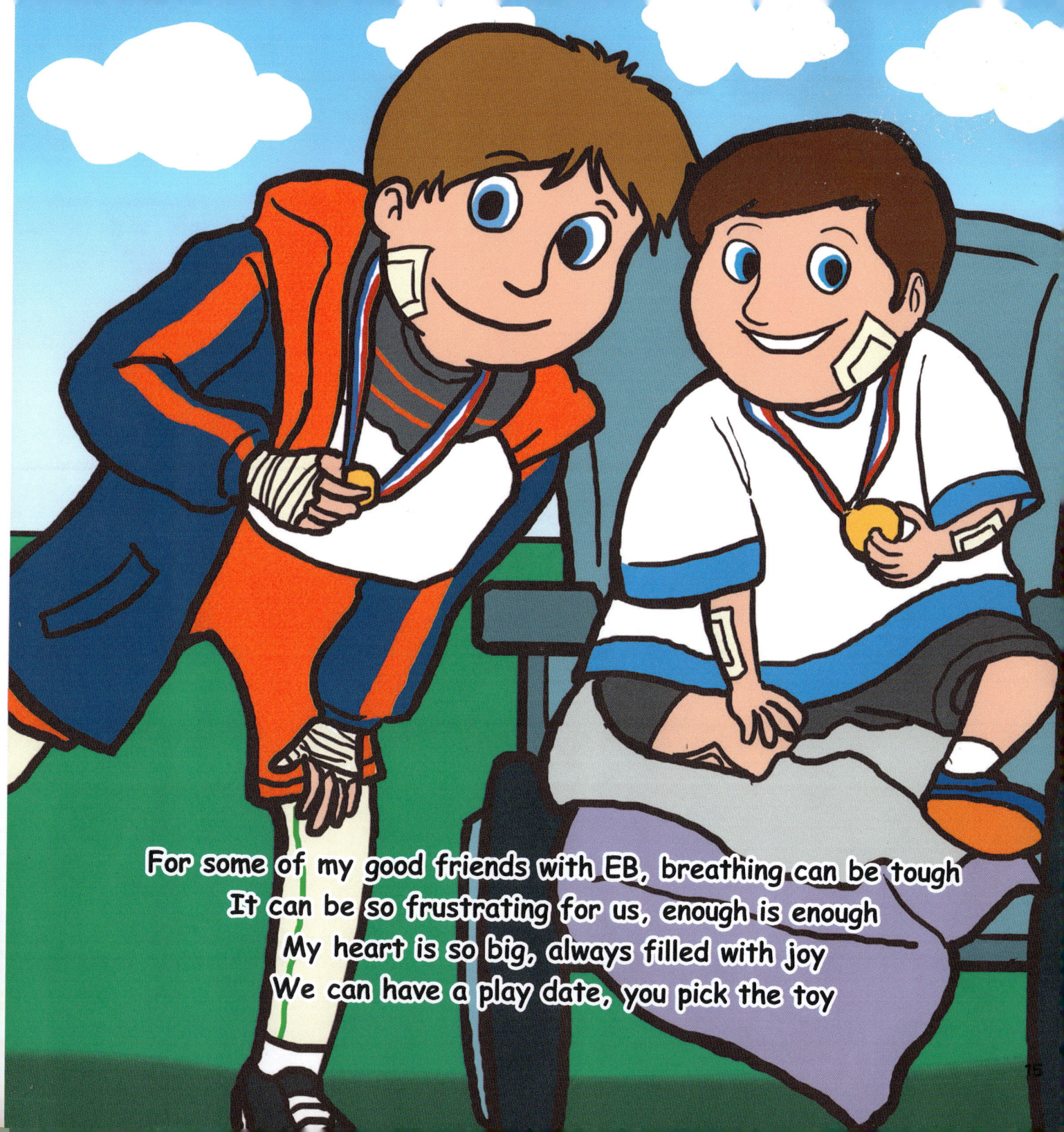

For some of my good friends with EB, breathing can be tough
It can be so frustrating for us, enough is enough
My heart is so big, always filled with joy
We can have a play date, you pick the toy

My skin itches so much, all I want to do is scratch
Don't worry, my disorder you will not catch
Music to my ears is a beautiful sound
A wheelchair may be needed to move around

I can read and write, I love to sing
I am able to do almost anything
Sports and hobbies, you pick the game
Don't feel sorry for me, Ryan is my name

So to all this powerful
message I must send,
If you give a child with EB a chance,
you will want to be their friend

Getting to Know Someone with Epidermolysis Bullosa (EB):"Children with EB are often called 'Butterfly Children.' Their skin is as fragile as a butterfly's wings because it is missing the 'glue' that normally holds it together. This makes it really easy for people with EB to get boo-boo's." (Denise Summers)

Some important questions you might ask as a friend:

I love sitting next to you at lunch. Can I share my potato chips with you?

We can be the best of friends, but sharing food with me is not always safe. Some crunchy and hard foods like potato chips can hurt my mouth and throat. Sometimes I'm on a special diet, too.

Why don't I always see you in class, P.E., or recess?

EB is tough on my skin and my insides, and sometimes I just don't feel good. Sometimes I'm hot, itchy, need my pads adjusted, or I don't have enough energy to be in class all day long with you.

It's wintertime...how come I have to wear my jacket outside, and you don't?

Since I have EB, I need special pads and bandages to keep me safe and to help me heal. The pads make me hot and it is like wearing extra layers of clothing. So, even though it might seem cold to you, it might be uncomfortable and hot for me.

Why can't you just use Band-Aids for your Boo-Boos?

My skin is extra fragile, just like a butterfly's wings. I can get boo-boos very easily. Band-Aids can hurt my skin because they are really sticky.

I want to give you a high-five. Is it safe?

One of my favorite things is being just like you, and I love to get gentle high-fives, fist-bumps and hugs. The best way to do this is to **ask me first**, and if you're not sure what to do, let me high-five YOU! (Denise Summers)

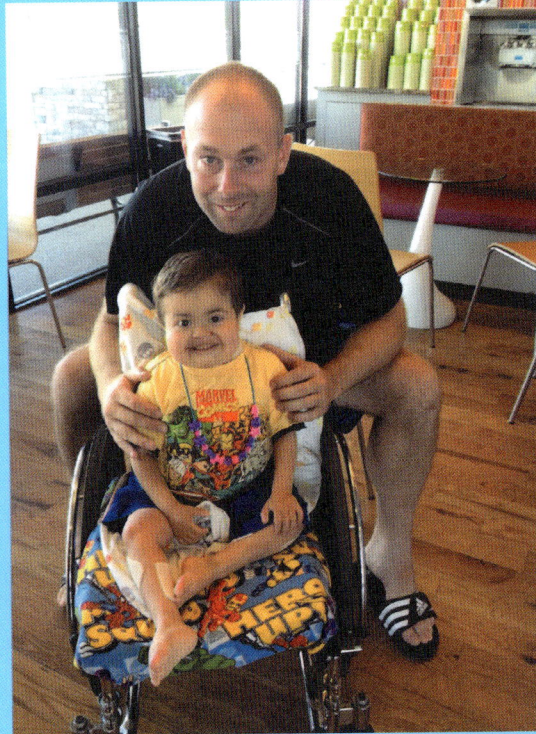

"The following book is dedicated to Ryan Summers. Ryan is an incredible boy that has many unique qualities. His positive attitude, exceptional personality, and great sense of humor are an inspiration to all."

15441202R00015

Printed in Great Britain
by Amazon